Rhinebeck
and the History
of the Landsman Kill Mills

Rhinebeck
and the History
of the Landsman Kill Mills

∼

John R. Conklin

EPIGRAPH BOOKS
RHINEBECK, NEW YORK

Rhinebeck and the History of the Landsman Kill Mills © Copyright 2019 by John R. Conklin

All rights reserved. No part of this book may be used or reproduced in any manner without written permission from the author except in critical articles or reviews. Contact the publisher for information.

Book design by Colin Rolfe

Paperback ISBN 978-1-948796-90-3

Library of Congress Control Number: 2019913707

Epigraph Books
22 East Market Street, Suite 304
Rhinebeck, NY 12572
(845) 876-4861
epigraphps.com

CONTENTS

Chapter 1	Introduction	1
Chapter 2	Research Problems	3
Chapter 3	The Mill Builders	5
Chapter 4	History of the Water Wheel	8
Chapter 5	The Millwright	12
Chapter 6	Industry on The Landsman Kill	14
Chapter 7	The Grist Mill	16
Chapter 8	Sources of Millstones	19
Chapter 9	The Saw Mill	21
Chapter 10	The Paper Mill	24
Chapter 11	The Gypsum Mill	25
Chapter 12	The Textile Mills	26
Chapter 13	The Oil Mill	28
Chapter 14	Vanderburgh Cove Mill; 1709	29
Chapter 15	The Upper Mill; 1715–1868	34
Chapter 16	The Rutsen/Schuyler/Miller Mills; 1739–1858	39
Chapter 17	The Lower Mill; 1750–1869	41
Chapter 18	The Montgomery/Ellerslie/Van Steenbergh Mills; 1774–1918	45
Chapter 19	The Isaac Davis Mill; 1790–1821	55
Chapter 20	The Wurtemburg Mill; 1790	58
Chapter 21	Buttermilk Falls Mill	62
Chapter 22	The Schuyler Mills; ?–1888	64
Chapter 23	The Forbes Saw Mill	67
Chapter 24	The Important Miller	69
Chapter 25	Fire Hazards	70
Chapter 26	Social Life at the Mills	71

Chapter 27	The Rhinebeck Millstone	74
Chapter 28	Millstones Today	77
Appendices		
	A. Casper Landsman	82
	B. Deeds and the Upper Mill	84
	C. A case for the date of the Upper Mill	86
References		88
About the Author		89

Old Mill Wheel.

CHAPTER 1

Introduction

The Landsman Kill meanders through the center of the Village of Rhinebeck on its six-mile journey to Vanderburgh Cove and the Hudson River. This tiny stream, barely ten feet wide and two feet deep, was the economic engine that powered the growth and prosperity of the Rhinebeck community in the 1700s. This little stream powered the water wheels that ground the grain, sawed the wood, made paper, gypsum, and cloth for the early inhabitants of Rhinebeck.

Rhinebeck was fortunate to have the wealth of the Beekman and Livingston families to provide the capital to erect the mills and hire the skilled workers to operate them. In addition to capital, an enterprise needs a market ready for its product or service. In the mid-1700s, Rhinebeck was the fastest growing area of Dutchess County, thanks to the Beekmans' energetic recruiting of leaseholders. There were thirty families near the Landsman Kill in 1709[1] and the number would more than double with the arrival of the German Palatines a few years later. There was a ready market for the output of the mills: wood for shelter and grain for food and fodder.

Historians—from the contemporaneous Morse, Smith, Hasbrouck, and Strong (editor of the Rhinebeck Gazette newspaper), to contemporary Rhinebeck Historical Society members Nancy Kelly, David Miller, and Marilyn Hatch—have provided a wealth of information on the mills. Morse's book, "Historic Old Rhinebeck, Echoes of two centuries; a Hudson River and Post Road Colonial Town,"

1 Morse page 22

first published in 1908, is an excellent reference. Jacob H Strong became publisher of The Rhinebeck Gazette in 1907. He was an avid historian and published many pieces mentioning the mills as well as featuring articles by the Daughters of the American Revolution and prominent citizens. These newspaper articles were a valuable resource for this work. The Dutchess County Clerk's Office was the source of research into deeds covering property transactions. The Rhinebeck Historical Society's cache of old maps helped verify mill locations.

This effort is an attempt to compile and document, and perhaps expand, the knowledge of the mills that thrived 300 years ago. It will look at the owners and operators of the mills and examine the culture of the times.

CHAPTER 2

Research Problems

When trying to document events in 1710, the historian encounters multiple problems. Relying on the past written word is fraught with challenges from simple errors to conflicting data on the same subject. Even the local Historical Markers, erected to mark important parts of history, contain errors. For example, the Schuyler historical marker at the site of one of the early mills is in error. This Schuyler was not a General, as his father was, but a Colonel in the militia.

The Landsman Kill Historical Marker at the site of the Upper Mill suggests that a "Morgan" was an owner of a local mill. The man was

"Morgan Lewis," married to a Livingston, an accomplished politician and a military commander in both the Revolutionary War and the War of 1812. One could spend a lot of time looking for a mill owner named Morgan!

Added to the accuracy equation is the fact that mills changed ownership over time, changed name, and changed the product they produced. For example, an important Rhinebeck mill began as a grist mill and converted to a woolen mill and then a paper mill. One important mill site had fourteen different owners and was called by several different names. Counting the number of mills became complicated. These complications have led some historians to inflate the number of mills on the Landsman Kill.

This article will try to make a more factual count, but will be subject to the usual errors that challenge all researchers!

CHAPTER 3

The Mill Builders

Rhinebeck was fortunate to have a major concentration of wealthy patent-holders who were willing to invest in building mills. The Beekmans, Livingstons, Rutsens, and the Schuylers were all active investors. Often berated for their wealth, the mills could not have existed without them. They were, however, protective of their mill rights. When they sold property bordering the Landsman Kill their deeds restricted the new owners from operating mills.[1]

Judge Henry Beekman of Kingston (1652 - 1716), sometimes referred to as Col. Henry Beekman Sr., obtained his first land patent in 1697. He never lived in the Rhinebeck area. He seldom sold his properties, but was active in recruiting families to the area to lease his land. His patent covered much of what is now Rhinebeck. Beekman had three offspring, a son, Col. Henry Beekman (1687-1775), and two daughters, Cornelia and Catherine, who would inherit all his Rhinebeck properties and build mills.

The Schuyler patent, north of the Beekmans', contained most of the lands that became Red Hook. Robert Livingston, the Lord of the Manor at Clermont, controlled most of what is now Columbia County. Their offspring were active investors, and through intermarriage kept the mills under family control.

The Judge's son, Col. Henry Beekman, played an active role in populating his father's holdings around Rhinebeck. In 1721 he married Janet Livingston, who died a few years later at age 21 leaving a daughter Margaret as their only surviving offspring. Margaret

1 Morse page 434

married Robert Livingston, the Lord of the Manor at Clermont. Her father and husband died within one year of each other in 1775, leaving her one of the wealthiest women in the Colonies. In liberal Dutch tradition, Margaret included her six daughters in her distribution of wealth. Unlike the English tradition of primogeniture, with the oldest son inheriting all the property, she included all her daughters. She distributed her holdings before her death. She was a truly remarkable woman whose activities could fill a history book! All six of her daughters would inherit large tracts of land, marry well, and build estates along the east bank of the Hudson. Many would build mills.

This chart showing Margaret's ten surviving children and their spouses may help with following the tangled family relationships.

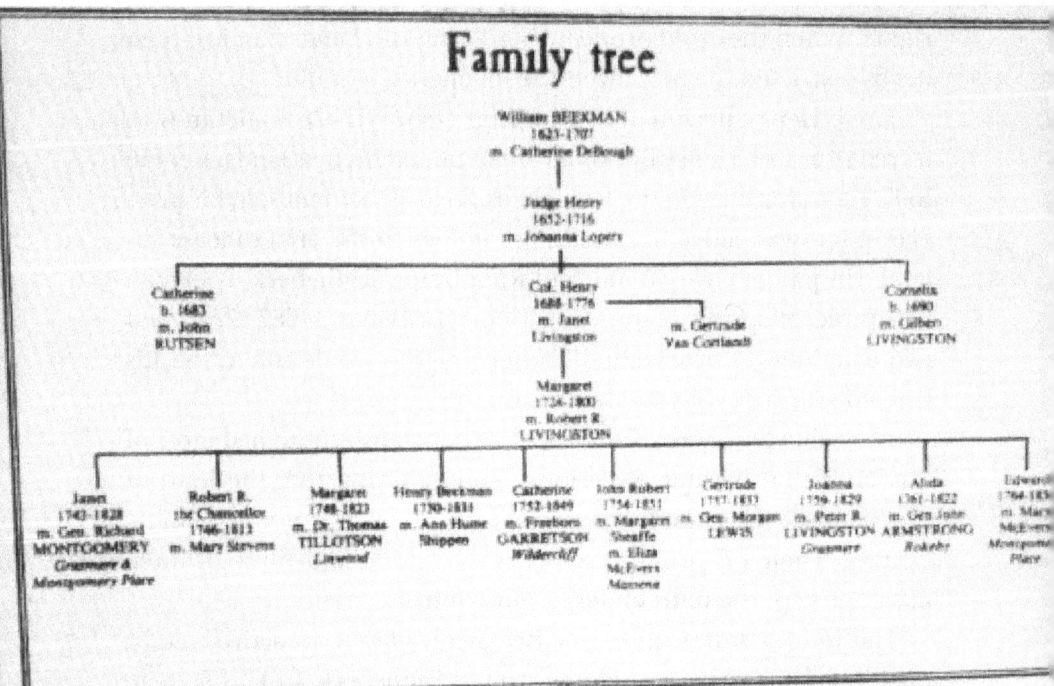

Judge Henry Beekman, the patentee from Kingston, with the help of Casper Landsman, an experienced miller, and William Traphagen, a wheelwright from Kingston, built the first mill in

Dutchess County. The mill was situated where the Landsman Kill falls through a waterfall into Vanderburgh Cove and the Hudson River Estuary. This mill location, with its dock on the Hudson, could attract business from Kingston as well as Rhinebeck.

The Landsman Kill is named for Casper Landsman, the first miller of the first mill.

Another mill builder was Jacob Rutsen, the son of Catherine Beekman and her husband John Rutsen. General Richard Montgomery and his Livingston wife, Janet, built a mill in 1774. General Morgan Lewis and his Livingston wife, Gertrude, owned three mills on the Landsman Kill.

All six of the earliest mills were financed by the Beekman and Livingston families.

An indication of the wealth these early mills generated is revealed in Col. Henry Beekman's will. It provided for his second wife, Gertrude Van Cortlandt:[2]

"From my mills at Rhinebeck yearly two barrels of fine flour, three barrels of bread, two barrels of Indian Corn meal, fifty barrels of bran and out of my orchard at Rhinebeck 10 barrels of the best fruit."

---

2 Gazette: Aug 8, 1921 Article "Mrs. Gertrude Von Cortlandt Beekman"

CHAPTER 4

History of the Water Wheel

Up until the perfection of the steam engine by James Watt in 1775, the only source of power was 1) animal – (horse, mule, or man), 2) wind – (Holland's wind mills), or 3) water-power – (the water wheel). Later, in 1838, an American patent was granted to Samuel B Howd[1] for a metal water turbine. This invention made the wooden water wheel obsolete. But up to this point in history, the wooden water wheel was the only source of water-power. The photo below shows a water turbine installed in a grist mill on the waters of the Shekomeko Creek near Pine Plains, NY.

1 Britannica https://www.britannica.com/technology/waterwheel_engines

History of the Water Wheel

The water wheel and water-power have a long history. The Roman historian, Vitruvius, an architect and engineer, documented a water wheel-powered grist mill in the 1st century BC[2]. By the Middle Ages, thousands of water-powered mills were operating throughout Europe. The early arrivals to this country brought this knowledge of the mills and the skills needed to build them. The first water-powered mill in the U.S. was built in 1640 in the Plymouth Colony in Massachusetts.

There are three types of water wheels; they are defined by where the force of water contacts the buckets of the wheel. If the water flows on top of the wheel, it is called an "Overshot," if it strikes in the middle, it is a "Breast Shot," if at the bottom of the wheel, it is called an "Undershot."

---

2 ibid.

Overshot – 60 to 70% efficiency[3]
Breast Shot – 40 to 60% efficiency
Undershot – 15 to 30% efficiency

  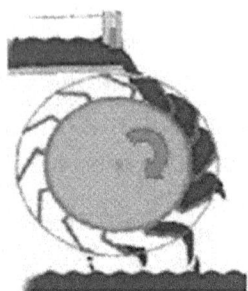

Undershot **Breastshot** Overshot

The most efficient is the "Overshot," and this type is most common on the Landsman Kill.

The wheel is typically made of oak with the number of compartments or buckets determined by the diameter of the wheel. The larger the diameter, the more power it can produce, but the more water-power it needs to turn the wheel. The shaft of the water wheel is extended several feet to reach inside the walls of the mill house. Attached to the shaft, inside the mill house, is a large face gear that engages a pinon gear. This transfers the direction of the rotary motion from horizontal to vertical and increases the speed of the spindle relative to the water wheel. This rotary motion can be

---

3 https://www.engr.psu.edu/mtah/articles/colonial_wood_water.htm

configured to drive a variety of tools, from rotating millstones to reciprocating saws and hammers.

Flowing water has energy and can be harnessed and directed to produce power. In simple terms, a column of water one-foot high exerts a pressure of 0.433 psi. and the amount of available pressure is called "head." In practice, "head" is the difference in height between the water surface upstream and the water surface downstream.

Flowing water also exerts pressure which can be measured. With these two measurements, "head" in feet and flowing water in cubic feet per second, the amount of water-power available can be calculated. As a simple rule of thumb, the diameter of the water wheel is equal to "head" minus two feet.

The earliest mill sites took advantage of a waterfall to provide the needed "head." A dam at the top of the falls created a pond which acted as a reserve for dry spells. Almost all the waterfalls on the Landsman Kill became mill sites.

CHAPTER 5

~

The Millwright

The skills to build a mill house, the water wheel, and the gearing belong to the millwright. The first employed by Judge Henry Beekman was William Traphagen, described as a "wheelwright" from Kingston.

Traphagen's design for his first mills is described by Morse in his history of Rhinebeck.[1] He describes an oblong frame building about 30 by 40 feet, two stories in height, with a peaked roof and a large "overshot" wheel on the end gable; double doors in front on each floor; a block and fall on the second-floor front. Depictions of mills on early maps show a two-story design.

1 Morse page 270

The Millwright

The millwright's responsibilities included the design of the water wheel and the gearing to connect the driving shaft to the millstones or the saw blade. After establishing the diameter of the wheel by the available water source (head plus cubic feet of flow), the millwright designs the gearing to meet the purpose of the mill. In a typical grist mill, the rotating millstone should turn at 100 to 120 rpm. A typical water wheel turns 10 to 20 rpm. From this the millwright will determine the number of teeth for the two gears.

CHAPTER 6

Industry on The Landsman Kill

From the very first mill built around 1709, a number of industries used the Landsman Kill.[1] Not all these activities required the water wheel and water-power. They will not be covered in this article.

Industries like the chair factory, ice harvesting, a cooperage, a tannery, and a distillery or two were all active at one time using the resources of the stream.

Activities that required power that could be provided by a water wheel include the grist mill for grinding various grains, the saw mill for lumber and paper-making, oil mills for vegetable oils for cooking and industrial use, textile mills – both the carding mill and the fulling mill – and gypsum mills for fertilizer and plaster. All these activities are part of the history of the Landsman Kill.

The early mills were predominantly the grist mill and the saw mill. In later years, entrepreneurs added oil, paper, and woolen mills but with various degrees of financial success. Following the imposition of tariffs on imported textiles by the U.S. Government in the 1840s, there was an economic reason to convert the mills from grinding grain to carding wool and cotton. Some mills of the Landsman Kill followed suit.

The grist mill was important and most prevalent because the landowners required their tenants to pay the rent in wheat and required them to use the landowner's mills. This requirement was part of Judge Henry Beekman's lease agreement and as late as the 1830s, General Morgan Lewis's leases included the wheat payments. Of

1 RHS files. Rhinebeck Gazette—0209.pdf. Article "The Old Post Road" by Mr. Harry Best—DAR

course this requirement ended with the "rent wars" and the legislation that followed. This legislation, enacted in 1846, may be another factor in the decline of the mills.

CHAPTER 7

The Grist Mill

Wheat was the most valuable commodity for the mill owner. His tenants were required to pay their yearly rent in bushels of wheat. There was a ready market for flour, both domestic and foreign. During the Napoleonic wars in Europe in the early 1800s, the price of wheat flour nearly tripled from the usual $4 per barrel to $11.

Other grains that supplied the grist mill were corn, rye, and oats, corn for both human and animal consumption, oats for mostly animal use, and rye for alcohol production. (In the mid-1800s, a still was often associated with the grist mill operation.) The millers would advertise "custom" work from flour to feeds.

The grist mill ground the grains – wheat, corn, oats, rye – into a usable and salable product. Local farmers brought their harvest to the mill to pay the rent, for the miller's fee, or for their own use. The mandatory requirements made the grist mill the most important asset for the mill builder/investor.

At the heart of the grist mill were two identically sized and "dressed" millstones. One stone was stationary, called a "bed stone," and the other a "runner stone" that rotated above it. The "runner stone" was attached to a shaft that turned through complicated gearing attached to the water wheel.

The surface of both stones was cut or dressed with deep grooves (furrows) with adjoining flat surface (lands). The grooves provided a cutting edge and helped move the product outward towards the discharge area. The runner stone could be adjusted up and down by a hoisting device. The dressing of the millstone was the job of the miller and each miller had his favorite pattern of lands and furrows.

The quality of the millstone, basically the hardness of the material, determined the amount of wear and how often the stone needed to be re-cut or dressed. A dull millstone was not efficient.

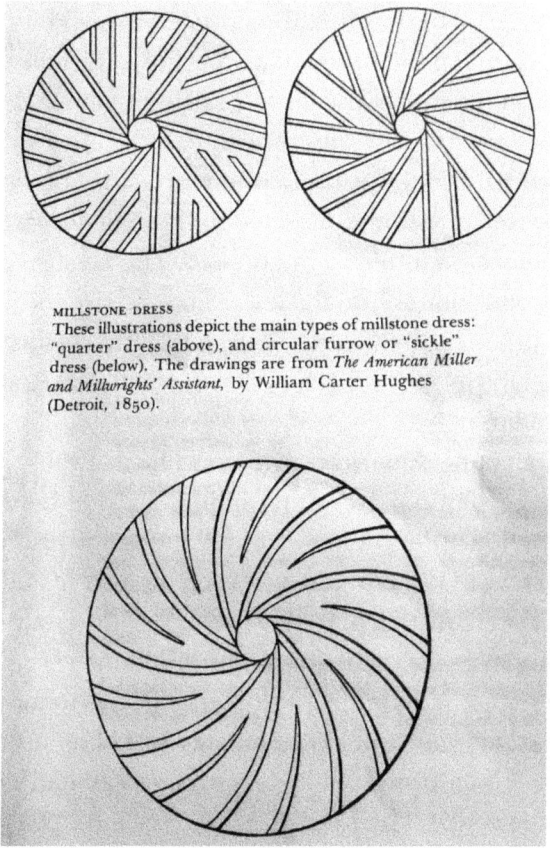

MILLSTONE DRESS
These illustrations depict the main types of millstone dress: "quarter" dress (above), and circular furrow or "sickle" dress (below). The drawings are from *The American Miller and Millwrights' Assistant*, by William Carter Hughes (Detroit, 1850).

A typical grist mill was laid out vertically, with the grain fed from the top (usually on the second floor) and the finished flour taken out the bottom. Ingenious devices, built mostly from wood, attempted to automate the operation. The grain was fed from a large hopper, through a feed tube, to the millstones. The rate of feed was controlled by an attachment to the rotating shaft holding the runner stone called a "damsel." The faster the shaft turned the greater the amount of feed. A typical rotating speed of 120 rpm was adjusted by the gearing and the flow of water to the water wheel. The finished flour was discharged to a sifter or "bolting" device that screened out oversized material. Once the mill was started, it would operate with only minor adjustments

The flow of water to power the water wheel was controlled by a "sluice" or "race". This was usually a wooden trough built to connect the source – a mill pond or top of a waterfall – with the water wheel. The miller could regulate the flow by raising a gate in the sluice box to adjust the speed of the water wheel.

The usual grist mill was housed in a two-story building. The upper floor housed the storage bins and the bolting device that cleaned the grain before it was fed to the hopper. The finished product was sent to a second "bolter," on the lower floor, to size the flour, usually into three products, grits, fine flour, and bran, before going into the barrels. Gravity was utilized to flow the material from storage to finished product.

In 1787, a young American inventor, Oliver Evans, developed a system that revolutionized grain milling.[1] In 1790 he was awarded a patent, the fourth in the new United States, for his invention. As President, George Washington approved the patent and immediately had the system installed at his Mount Vernon estate. It is still in operation today as part of the museum at Mount Vernon. Evans employed a system of continuous belts with pockets to move the grain and flour around the mill. He automated a cooling process to keep the warm material from spoiling. This improvement, however, was eighty years after Beekman built his first mill in 1709. The early mill builders did not have the advantage of this labor-saving method.

The size of the millstone determined its capacity to grind flour: a 46-inch diameter stone was rated at 300 pounds per hour, a 48-inch at 400 lbs/hr, and a 55-inch at 500 lbs/hr.

---

1 https://www.asme.org/topics-resources/content/oliver-evans

CHAPTER 8

Sources of Millstones

There was a major millstone manufacturing operation in the Shawangunk area of Ulster County beginning in 1732. Before that time all millstones were imported from Europe, specifically England, Germany, or France. So the millstones for the very first Beekman mills were European. By the time of the Revolutionary War, when commerce with Europe was interrupted, it was necessary to have a local source.

The stone industry in Ulster County was in full development by the late 1700s. This included cut stone for buildings, stone quarried for the cement industry, and granite for millstones. The center of the millstone industry was around High Falls. The grey-colored granite came from the Shawangunk mountain range and the stones were shipped from the Rondout waterfront of Kingston.

This area was the largest center for the production of millstones in the entire country. They were called "Esopus" stones. The Gem and Mineral Society refers to the material as "Shawangunk Quartz Conglomerate" and this type of granite has been identified as the material in Rhinebeck area millstones. As late as 1880, Ulster County boasted six millstone dealers in Accord, two in Alligerville, and one in Kyserike.

A source for sandstone material for local stones was located near Mt. Tom in Connecticut, just across the Dutchess County line. A sandstone grindstone, not a mill stone, most likely from Mt. Tom, has been found in the Rhinebeck area.

The best and most expensive millstones are the French "Burr" stones. They are a composite of hard, long-lasting material formed by cementing a fresh water-formed granite into the shape of the millstone. The advantage of this stone is that it does not have to be dressed as frequently as the Esopus stones. Note the price difference between the imported Burr stone and the local Esopus stone.

Prices of Millstones from Mr. Tyack ☐

	French Burrs			Esopus Millstones	
Sizes	Prices	Weight	Sizes	Prices	Weight
2ft.	$35	350#	1 ft. 6in.	$18	300#
2ft. 6in.	$45	450#	2ft.	$2	400
3ft.	$90	570#	2ft. 6in.	$35	550
3ft. 6in.	$120	1160#	3ft.	$30	650
4ft.	$130	2000#	3ft. 6in.	$35	850
4ft. 4in.	$135	2420#	4ft.	$45	1600
4ft. 6in.	$145	2800#	4ft. 4in.	$50	2150
5ft.	$200	3260#	4ft. 6in.	$55	2800
5ft. 6in.	$225	3600#	5ft.	$90	3600

Millstone prices (1848)
From University of Virginia Archives, MS 3490

CHAPTER 9

The Saw Mill

The saw mill provided the building materials for the fast-growing population of Rhinebeck. The arrival of 35 families of Palatines—from the disastrous experiment of harvesting naval stores at Livingston's Clermont—and their need for shelter created an added incentive for the mill builder.

The water-powered saw mill replicated the old manual method of sawing logs, in which a two-man team used a "pit" dug into the earth, or a raised platform, to move the metal saw up and down. The man below was called the "pit man," who pulled the saw down, while the man on top pulled the saw back up. This up/down motion was duplicated in the water-powered mill.

The water wheel was connected to an eccentric gear, revolving in an elliptical motion, moving the saw up and down. The shaft connecting the gear to the saw was called the "pitman" after the name of the old manual team member.

Marilyn Hatch, a former member of the Rhinebeck Historical Society with an expert's knowledge of the workings of a saw mill, describes the method of moving the log to be cut:

> "There is a lever system that is attached to a wooden frame, called the sash, that holds the saw blade in place. As the saw blade is pushed up by the pitman arm, the lever system transfers the energy to the carriage to move it forward into the blade for the next downward stroke to make the next cut. The carriage only moves forward during the upward stroke of the blade. Depending on the type of wood being cut the carriage moves forward from 1/4" for hardwood, such as oak, up to 1" for a softwood such as pine. The up and down motion of the saw is 120 rpm."

The Saw Mill

Marilyn is an officer of Scribner's Mill Preservation, Inc. in Harrison, Maine, which has restored and is operating a water-powered saw mill.

This arrangement effectively automated the process. One man, with a boy helper, could produce 1000 feet of pine boards per day. Compare this to the manual team that averaged twelve pine boards a day.

The saw blade, as shown in the nearby photo, was a metal piece in the same configuration as the saw used in the two-man effort. The first circular saw did not appear until 1814. The band saw was patented in 1869. It is not known if any of these improvements were incorporated in Rhinebeck's later saw mills.

An 1840 U.S. Census reported 31,650 saw mills in the United States.[1]

---

1 See Chapter 4 note #2. engr.psu.edu/

CHAPTER 10

The Paper Mill

Papermaking in Colonial America used cloth rags, hemp, cotton, or linen, but not wool or wood, as the raw material for the paper.

The water wheel provided power to "hammer" the wet rags into a pulp-type slurry. The wheel was connected to a rotating shaft that used "cams" to raise and lower the "hammer." Later improvements featured a "beater," a rotating cylinder with macerating blades that broke the fibers into pulp.

The pulp slurry was transferred to a set of screens, that after de-watering, left a residue on the screen surface, which, when dried, produced a sheet of paper. Paper made from rags was very strong, durable, and hard to tear. Control of color was a problem. The rags were sorted and graded by color. The dark rags were often bleached to improve the color. The best grade of paper was used for writing paper, the second grade was used for newsprint, and the final grade for wrapping paper.

Straw was used for pulp when making brown paper. The Rhinebeck upper mill at Crystal Lake experimented with using bamboo fibers. It was reported to be too difficult to source and the trial was not successful.

The use of wood chips came in to practice after two German engineers, in 1843, developed a method for their use as pulp. This process used heat and acid to break the fibers and was not part of the Landsman Kill industry.

One of the early paper mills (not on the Landsman Kill) named their finished product "HammerMill" bond. The Hammermill Paper Company is still with us today. Now you know where the name came from!

CHAPTER 11

The Gypsum Mill

Gypsum is a relatively soft, rock-like material that, when ground to a powder, can be used in fertilizer and in plaster.

The mineral is called a hydrous calcium sulfate. Its chemical composition is $CaSO_4 \cdot 2H_2O$. It looks like chalk and is mined or quarried. The usual process involves quarrying, crushing, and grinding to a fine powder.

The water wheel powers a rolling crusher similar to the device shown in the photo.

CHAPTER 12

The Textile Mills

THE CARDING MILL

"Carding" is a mechanical process that straightens and aligns fibers so they can be spun into yarn or thread to be woven into textiles. Both cotton and wool are "carded."

The straightening is done by a carding machine. The design is a large rotating drum, surrounded by multiple smaller rollers. The drum is covered with a "carding cloth" covered with metal pins or teeth, which engage the fibers. As the drum rotates, the pins pull the strands apart and align them into a "skein."

If the material is very fine, such as wool, the number of pins in the carding cloth is increased. The coarser the material the lower the number of pins. The "TPI," teeth per inch, for fine wool ranges from 72 to 112.

The machine is powered through the water wheel.

The Textile Mills

This drum carder was invented in 1748 by Lewis Paul in Birmingham, England. George Booth, about 1803, operating a mill in Poughkeepsie, NY, is credited with bringing the first carding machine into the United States.[1] Textile manufacturing presented a profitable opportunity after the tariffs of 1840 and the demand for uniforms during the Civil War.

A Rhinebeck business directory, published in 1867, lists a Matthew Michell as a manufacturer of Carding cloth.

THE FULLING MILL

A "Fulling" mill works with wool as the raw material. Fulling is a term to describe the process of compacting wool to make it more dense or "full." Also known as "tucking" or "walking," it is a step in making woolen cloth. This step was originally carried out by the pounding of the woolen cloth by the fuller's feet or hands, or a club.

The cloth is thickened by matting the fibers together to give it strength and increase its water resistance. An example of fulling is the making of felt, a dense, compact, water-resistant material.

The water wheel powers the "pounding" devices similar to those used in papermaking.

The machine is operated by cams driven by the shaft of the water wheel. Sometimes called a "tappet" wheel, it lifts and drops the hammers.

This process was developed in Persia in the 5th century BC. It migrated from Islamic Spain to Western Europe in the 11th and 12th centuries. The first mention of a fulling mill is from 1066 in France's Normandy.

---

1 Hank Hasbrouck. *The History of Dutchess Country, New York*. P 236

CHAPTER 13

~

The Oil Mill

The Oil Mill crushed and pressed oil-bearing seeds to extract a vegetable oil.

Typical seeds were rapeseed, sunflower, cotton, caster, soybean, grape, flax, and corn. The result was a vegetable oil for foodstuff, cooking, cattle feed, or an oleochemical used as a lubricant.

CHAPTER 14

Vanderburgh Cove Mill
1709

By 1709 there were thirty families in the Rhinebeck area. A grist mill and a saw mill were needed to serve this market.

Judge Henry Beekman (1652-1716) built the first mill on the Landsman Kill. The location was a cove on the Hudson River where the Landsman Kill flows over a fifty-foot waterfall into the Hudson estuary. He built a dam, a grist mill, a saw mill, and a dock.

Judge Beekman was a prominent and wealthy Dutchman. He was born and died in Kingston. His father, William Beekman, arrived in New Amsterdam with Peter Stuyvesant in 1647. William married Catalina de Boogh and after several assignments from Stuyvesant, moved to Kingston. Their son, Henry, became a Judge and representative of the Colonial Government under the English Governor and acquired large tracts of land in Dutchess County. Judge Beekman owned most of the lands that became Rhinebeck. His property extended from Vanderburgh Cove east of the Landsman Kill to the Schuyler patent at Red Hook.

An earlier patent was awarded to five Dutchmen from Kingston, Arie Roosa, John Van Wagenen, Gerrit Artsen, and two Kip brothers. This patent covered land from Vanderburgh Cove west of the Landsman Kill to the Hudson River and east to Rhinebeck. The Landsman Kill was the property line between the two patents, a situation that would later precipitate a flurry of land sales to ensure ownership of the mill sites.

The date of this first mill was prior to 1710. How much earlier cannot be determined. Most historical records list the date of this mill as 1710, but it appears to have been built earlier. The records state Judge Beekman built a dam, grist mill, saw mill, and a dock. This date is based on a Beekman land purchase dated 1710. The details in this deed are some interesting material.[1]

Beekman owned property on the east side of the Kill, while Roosa owned the property on the west side with valuable Hudson River access. It is possible Beekman built his mill without regard to Roosa's ownership. In 1710, Judge Henry's son, Col. Henry Beekman, bought six acres from Arie Roosa, "to begin 100 yards North of the mill dam already in existence." One can speculate that this was a land dispute settled by the son as a mediator. This would not be the only time a mill was built before the property lines were confirmed. There is evidence that the next mill the team of Beekman, Traphagen, and Landsman built also had an issue with property rights.

This Cove site, with access to the Hudson River, could support business activity from both Kingston and Rhinebeck. It was an ideal site for the first mills. The dock was an important asset. Judge Beekman was reported to have a valuable family connection with the docks of the West India Company in New York. His grandfather, Wilhelmus, had a financial interest in the company. There was a "brisk" river trade with New York. A deed dated 1716 between Gerrit Artsen and his son-in-law Hendricus Heermance makes reference to Beekman's "corn mill."

The Judge deeded this property to his son, Colonel Henry Beekman, in 1713, perhaps for his assistance as mediator in the first land dispute over the boundaries of the Landsman Kill.

Judge Beekman employed Casper Landsman, an experienced mill operator, to select mill sites on the stream. Casper was a German Palatine, part of the migration to Livingston's Clermont to harvest "naval stores." His name was originally spelled "Caspar

---

1 Gazette. Sept 10, 1880. Article "The History of Rhinebeck" Roads & Mills

Lampman."[2] The first name for the stream, appearing in early deeds, was "Lantsman," however the stream's name would eventually become known as the Landsman Kill. All historians agree it was named after Casper.

The mill structure was built by William Traphagen. In a 1710 legal document, Traphagen is referred to as "wheelwright from Kingston." He was an early business associate of Judge Beekman's. In 1705 Traphagen purchased 280 acres from Beekman that made up the western part of today's Rhinebeck.

The main purpose of a grist mill is to grind wheat into flour. The Beekman leases required rent payments in schepels of wheat. Typical rents were one schepel of good winter wheat per acre per year to be paid to the miller each spring.[3] A schepel was equal to ¾ of a bushel of wheat. The farmer was required to use Beekman's mills, not only for rent payments, but for the farmer's own needs. The saw mill produced the pine boards needed for houses and barns.

In 1779, Dr. Thomas Tillotson acquired the mill properties. He purchased adjacent land from Isaac Van Etten and built a river-view estate called "Linwood." Thomas Tillotson, a Surgeon General during the Revolutionary War, was married to Margaret Livingston, one of the elder Margaret's six daughters.

In 1812, William Schell leased the property and operated a saw mill and a distillery.[4] Tillotson died in 1832 when the mill property was bought by Dr. Federal Vanderburgh, a pioneer of Homeopathy medicine. The cove on which the mill was located was named for him.

There is no record of when the mill ceased operation. In a deed description involving another mill site, today's Mill Road was called "the road from the Post road to Dr Vandenbergh's mills." The date of that document was 1857, so the mill was still in existence, but perhaps not operating.

2 Verbal conversation. Nancy Kelly. Jan 31, 2019. See Addendum A.
3 The Emich Family of Thunder Mountain. https://www.familysearch.org/service/records/storage/das_mem/patron
4 Morse page 58

The picturesque waterfall, where the Landsman Kill drops down to the cove, is shown below.

Archaeological remains of the mill's foundation can be seen at low tide. An abandoned millstone graces the area. The west side of the site shows evidence of beams that once projected from the wall abutment out over the stream. This may have been for a dock or a method of supporting the mill itself. Rocks, visible in the photo, are most likely remains of the mill foundation.

Vanderburgh Cove Mill—1709

The millstone, perhaps 300 years old, is a bed stone, 55 inches in diameter. This stone is capable of producing 500 pounds of fine flour per hour.

CHAPTER 15

The Upper Mill
1715–1868

This mill site is near the "Flatts," as the emerging and expanding commercial center of Rhinebeck was then called. The "Flatts" competed with "Pinks Corner," or the "Kerchhoek," the original settlement of the Palatines, two miles to the northeast. A highway historical plaque marks the location of "Old Rhinebeck" near the site of the restored Palatine house.

The Upper Mill—1715

The dam at the top of the falls created a large pond, at first called the mill pond, then Asher's lake, then Crystal Lake, and now Legion Park. The lake and the Landsman Kill parallel South Street, with many home sites bordering the water. It is a pleasant part of Rhinebeck Village.

This mill was built with Judge Henry Beekman's funds by millwright William Traphagen and it was operated by miller Casper Landsman. The date is recorded as 1715. The 1715 date first published by and attributed to Morse has been questioned by local historians. In particular an exchange of property in 1719, between the sons of the two men, Col. Henry Beekman and William Traphagen, who initiated the original sale of 281 acres in 1705, called into question the date of the mill.

A further look into the actions of the principals in the late 1700s and a review of the actual deeds will help shed some light on this complex problem. It appears that this mill, like the Vanderburgh Mill, was built on land of questionable ownership.

The property line of the 1686 Beekman patent was the east bank of the Landsman Kill, with the Dutchman of Kingston owning the tract from the west bank of the Landsman Kill to the Hudson River. To further complicate the picture, Beekman, in 1705, sold 281 acres to William Traphagen with the property line as the west side of the Landsman Kill. This property included land that would become the Upper Mill site. The deed for this transaction is recorded in the very first book of deeds in the Dutchess County Clerk's Office, Liber 1, page 380.

In 1719, Beekman's son rectified the problem of the Upper Mill by buying six acres from Traphagen to include "the sale of water for convenience to erect mills thereon." As with the Vanderburgh Cove land purchases, the deed describes this transaction with reference to the existing mill dam. The 1719 deed is accompanied by a map clearly showing the presence of a mill. The new property lines are described as " beginning at the falls near the Mill dam," also acknowledging the existence of the mill prior to 1719. So it appears that the Upper Mill was in existence before 1719.

Judge Beekman enlisted the services of Casper Landsman, a Palatine miller, and William Traphagen, a Kingston wheelwright, to participate in his mills project. Traphagen designed the mill building, as described by Morse, and built the gearing associated with a water wheel-driven mill. Casper Landsman was supposed to have selected the sites and operated the mills. This is the same team that built the first mill at the cove.

Henry Beekman, in 1715, recruited 35 palatine families to lease his lands in the Rhinebeck area. The typical lease terms required the tenant to pay Beekman, each year, one schepel of winter wheat for each acre of leased land. Beekman needed a local mill to process his wheat. The Vanderburgh Cove location was too distant from Pink's Corners. The presence of these 35 families support the argument that the mill was built in 1715.

The 1715 date, as reported by Morse and Hasbrouck, is most likely correct. For more background on the preponderance of evidence to support the 1715 date, see Appendix C.

A detailed summary of the deeds in question can also be found in Appendix B.

The Upper Mill—1715

The Beekman and Livingston clan continued to operate the mill until 1847 when Peter R. Livingston died. A 1797 Town of Rhinebeck map lists both the Upper and Lower Mills as owned by Mrs. Livingston. This would be Margaret Beekman Livingston, who inherited her father's property on his death in 1775. Peter R. Livingston, a cousin, married Margaret Beekman Livingston's daughter, Joanna, and acquired "Grasmere," a Rhinebeck estate, and the mills. The Livingston family controlled the mill for 132 years.

Hendrick Denker was the miller of the Upper Mill from 1735 until 1772.[1] The account books covering this period give a glimpse of the commercial activities in the mid-1700s. Denker was a slaveholder, and his account books have references to the names of "Prince," "Jack," "Little Sam," and "Little Purys." He did a large barter business, with tailors and shoemakers making clothes for his slaves, and blacksmiths and coopers providing services for his products. He had a long list of customers. Of interest, from 1756 to 1759, he trained an apprentice miller, Hendrick Tincker, for a fee of 22 Pounds per year. Denker's account book lists over 350 customers.

An interesting entry in 1752 notes that Van Fraidingburgy and William Hallaman "helped to ride a millstone from Esopus."[2]

Colonel Beekman, in his record book, remarks that 140 families came to the mill. In 1751, he built a new storehouse by the mill.[3] The mill was prospering through this period, before Beekman's death in 1775.

In the mill's 153-year history, it went from a grist mill, to a woolen mill, and finally to a paper mill.

Peter Livingston took over the mill property from Margaret Livingston, his mother-in-law. Upon Peter's death in 1847, the mill was sold to Richard R. Sylands and James Hogan.[4]

---

1 "Some Dutchess County, New York Early Residents, 1735–1772" by Kenneth Scott
2 Same as 1—"Denker"
3 RHS, Nancy Kelly. Edward Livingston Papers. Box 128
4 Morse page 55

Hogan was the initial paper mill operator. Timothy Baker was employed as the paper maker and was reported to be an experienced operator. Under Timothy Baker the mill produced a fine grade of white paper and a very thin tissue paper. Twenty years later, an 1867 Map of Rhinebeck lists Hogan operating a paper mill and manufacturing paper.

The mill experimented, unsuccessfully, with making paper from bamboo. The mill, in later years, was never very prosperous. It burned in 1868 and was never rebuilt.[5] The property became Legion Park, owned by the Village of Rhinebeck.

For a long while the old water wheel of the Upper Mill could be seen leaning against the bank of the Landsman Kill. It was featured on a local postcard. Crystal Lake is still a popular site for picnics, strolling, and fishing.

5 Morse page 60

CHAPTER 16

The Rutsen/Schuyler/Miller Mills
1739–1858

This property is located at the very eastern part of Rhinebeck, just a few yards east of present-day Route 9G. After the division of the Beekman holdings in 1737, Col. Henry and his two sisters, Catherine and Cornelia, became large landholders. Catherine married three times. Her marriage to Capt. John Rutsen (1690-1726) produced a son, Jacob Rutsen, who married his cousin, Alida Livingston, daughter of Cornelia and Gilbert Livingston. He married at age 21, and in 1737, the couple settled on Lot 2 of the old Beekman patent.

They built a grist mill near the falls of the Landsman Kill in 1739[1] or 1742, both dates are in the records. The mill was operated by Jacob and when he died in 1753 at age 37, the mill was owned by his son John Rutsen (1743-1771), who died at an early age. His widow, Phoebe Carman Rutsen married Robert Sands, who briefly became the mill owner. Philip J. Schuyler became the owner when he married John Rutsen's daughter Sarah.

[1] *Dutchess County Doorways 1730–1830* page 212 by Helen Wikiston Reynolds

The mill was constructed of stone and its location was in the vicinity of the bridge over the Landsman Kill on the road to the "Grove," the estate owned by the mill owners at respective times. The mill was torn down in 1858.[2] Of interest, the field stones from the Grist Mill were salvaged and used in the construction of the arched bridges on the Salisbury Turnpike, now Route 308.

The first miller was a man named Eighmy. He would later own his own mills and the location of Eighmyville is named for his efforts. From 1783 to 1788, John Ring was employed as the miller.[3] Ring would go on to run the Oriel Mills in Red Hook.

A saw mill was located upstream of the grist mill, near the falls. The dates of the operation of the saw mill are not available. A large mill pond was created above the falls and was known as the "saw mill pond." There is no record as to when the saw mills were abandoned. This site supported two mills.

A mill stone found nearby is a 48-inch runner stone and is shown in the photo alongside.

The mill pond is present today.

---

2 Gazette, Sept 20, 1936. Article "Historical Society Visits the Grove"
3 https://www.werelate.org/wiki/person:johannes_ring_(1)

CHAPTER 17

∼

The Lower Mill
1750–1869

The Lower Mill is located a short distance west and downstream of the Beekman Upper Mill, in the vicinity of what is now the parking lot of the Astor Home for Children.

It was built by William Traphagen, Jr in 1750.[1] The miller was Isaac Kole or Cool and a wooden beam in the mill carried the initials "1750 WT/IK." Isaac Cool was married to Traphagen's daughter, so it was a family venture. The miller's stone house was nearby and was a sentimental part of the history of Rhinebeck.

1 Gazette, Aug 29, 1908. Article "The Traphagen Grist Mill on the Flatts"

The grist mill was most likely financed by the Livingstons, as a 1797 map shows the Lower Mill as owned by Mrs. Livingston, the same Margaret Beekman Livingston who divided her lands among her six daughters long before her death.

Her son, Col. Henry Beekman Livingston became the owner of this grist mill upon his return from the Revolutionary War. He brought with him a soldier of the War by the name of Sgt. Daniel McCarty and installed him as the miller.

Col. Henry Beekman Livingston had a complex personality that eventually caused his estrangement from his family. He was an eager soldier, raised a local Regiment for the Revolutionary War, fought alongside Benedict Arnold at the battle of Saratoga, and was with Washington at Valley Forge. He was a friend of Lafayette and Baron Von Steuben. In 1778 he was in command of a successful rear guard action at the battle of Monmouth that turned a rout into a victory for Washington. The victory came at a high cost. His unit took heavy casualties.

Although a successful commander, he was arrogant, and was court-martialed for disrespecting a senior officer, a man he considered socially inferior. Perhaps his wartime experiences were caused by what today is known as Post Traumatic Stress Disorder. He exhibited erratic behavior, from a violent temper, to stalking his wife, to plowing his fields wearing silk dress clothing.

He owned two mills on the Landsman Kill.

By 1832, both the Lower Mill and the older Upper Mill were owned by Peter R. Livingston, the owner of Grasmere. Janet Livingston Montgomery, after her husband's death, sold the property to her sister, Joanna, who was married to her cousin Peter. The Livingston families controlled this property for 97 years.

When Peter R. Livingston died in 1847, the mill was offered for sale. The mill was purchased by John Ansell. The 1867 map listing the business of Rhinebeck shows John Ansell as proprietor of a flour and grist mill. He was the owner when it burned in 1869. The mill was never rebuilt.

Millers for the lower grist mill included the first miller, Isaac Cool, then Daniel McCarty, James Hobbs, who worked the mill for 30 years, Peter G. Quick, and finally John Ansell. This site has also been referred to, in the local newspaper, as the Traphagen Mill, the Hobbs Mill, and the Rhinebeck Mill.

Note in Ansell's advertisement he refers to the mill as "The Rhinebeck Mill" and calls attention to his new Burr millstone. This is the expensive, imported French stone that millers recognize as superior to the local Esopus stones. He is implying that it will produce a better product.

By this late date, water-powered mills were being replaced by steam power. An 1846 revision to the New York State Constitution, as a result of the Rent Wars, made tenant payments in wheat impractical. The Rent Wars were a reaction to the harsh terms of the lease agreements which required

RHINEBECK MILLS.

THE partnership heretofore existing between ANSELL & STANFORD having been dissolved by mutual consent, the business of the above Mills continues to be carried on by the subscriber, who will keep on hand for sale a supply of fresh ground

FLOUR, MEAL, FEED, &C.

☞ Orders left at the mills, or at JENNINGS' STORE in the village of Rhinebeck, will receive immediate attention.

CUSTOM GRINDING,

for Bakers, Merchants, Farmers and others, will be attended to with dispatch. A new Burr stone has recently been put up expressly for grinding feed, by which the operation is greatly facilitated and the work PERFORMED IN THE BEST POSSIBLE MANNER.

GRAIN OF ALL KINDS

wanted at the above Mills, for which the highest market prices will be paid. JOHN ANSELL.

Rhinebeck, Sept. 15, 1868.

the tenant to rent "in perpetuity" with no option to own the property. After a series of renters protests the New York State Assembly passed legislation in favor of the tenants. These two factors contributed to the demise of the water-powered grist mill.

The only archaeological remains at the Lower Mill site are a part of the stone foundation and a millstone. The millstone found at the site was donated by the Astor Home to the Quitman Resource Center and is on display at the Quitman House. It is not a Burr stone. The millstone is a bed stone, 57 inches in diameter and 8 inches thick.

The remains of the foundation are shown at stream side.

The Rhinebeck Millstone, found by the Highway Department in 2018, could possibly be from this mill site. It is also 57 inches in diameter, 8 inches thick. The dress, however, does not match the Astor Home millstone.

CHAPTER 18

The Montgomery/Ellerslie/Van Steenbergh Mills
1774–1918

This mill site is located at the waterfall below the mill pond formed by the junction of two Kills. I refer to this site as the "Twin Kills," as the names have changed over the course of its 144 years of history. The larger Landsman Kill is joined by the smaller Rhinebeck Kill below Sand Hill. The Rhinebeck Kill was referred to as the Kip Kill in early deeds. This mill was operating from 1774 until after 1918, the longest operation of any of the Landsman Kill mills. It is an important site, boasting a huge mill pond that could easily support two separate mills. This site incurred a fire and was rebuilt, with the new mill featuring innovations. It was the last operating grist mill on the Landsman Kill.

The east bank of the Landsman Kill was part of the Beekman patent (owned by Janet and Richard Montgomery) and the west bank was part of the Kipsbergen's Kip patent. Like the first two mill sites, this arrangement precipitated a lot of land sales aimed at control of the water rights.

The mill was built by Richard Montgomery in 1774, shortly after his marriage to Janet Livingston. They were the owners of part of the Beekman patent that would become Grasmere. He and Janet began construction of a house on the Grasmere property, which the General never saw completed. The project was interrupted when Montgomery was tapped by General George Washington to lead the ill-fated invasion of Canada. General Richard Montgomery was killed, New Year's Eve in 1775, storming the battlements at Quebec.

Not much is recorded about the operation of the Montgomery mill until 1785 when Col. Henry B. Livingston was operating a saw mill at the site. This is the second mill he owned upon his return from the War. In that same year, Livingston bought eleven acres on the west side of the Landsman Kill from the Kips and built a grist mill. Morse states the site also supported an oil mill.

General Morgan Lewis bought the mill from Henry Livingston in 1812.

Morgan Lewis was a prominent member of the Rhinebeck Community. He was a lawyer, politician, and military officer serving in both the Revolutionary War and as a General in the War of 1812. Lewis was elected Governor of the State of New York, serving from 1804 to 1807. He married Gertrude Livingston in 1779, one of the six daughters of Margaret Beekman Livingston.

What is interesting is the method Morgan Lewis used to acquire the property from his brother-in-law. Col. Henry Livingston sold the mill to Christian Schell in 1812.[1] Schell is credited with establishing "The Flatts" as the commercial center of Rhinebeck and he is commemorated by a historical marker on the corner of Market Street and the Post Road. Schell immediately turned the mill property over to Gen. Morgan Lewis. The wording of the deed acknowledges that Schell was purchasing on behalf of Lewis.

Col. Henry B. Livingston had a complicated relationship with his family. He was considered unstable and was vilified for the way he treated his wife and daughter. His mother, Margaret Beekman Livingston, took over the responsibility of raising his daughter. His sisters shunned all contact, labeling him the "black sheep" of the

---

1 Dutchess County Clerk. Liber 23. Pages 99, 117, 162

The Montgomery/Ellerslie/Van Steenbergh Mills—1774

Livingston family, perhaps the reason Morgan Lewis used an intermediator for the mill purchase.

The Lewis family controlled this site for 45 years, from 1812 until 1857.

General Lewis and Gertrude Livingston had only one offspring, a daughter named Margaret who married Maturin Livingston, a cousin. Margaret and Maturin acquired an 860-acre river estate and named it Ellerslie. This property extended from the Hudson River east to the Landsman Kill. In later years it was owned by businessman William Kelly and in 1895 by Levi P. Morton, Governor of New York and Vice President of the United States. Margaret, on the death of her father, became the owner of large tracts of the old Beekman patent, including the mill property.

In about 1812, Lewis rented the nearby Grasmere property and bought the mill site through the transaction with Christian Schell. In 1814, he acquired an additional 11 acres north of the Landsman Kill. By 1836, a survey of Lewis's mill property showed a total of 38 acres. When Lewis died in 1844, the mill was inherited by his only daughter, Margaret Lewis Livingston. Her husband, Maturin, was the brother of Peter R. Livingston, the owner of Grasmere and two mills near the Flatts. The mill site became known as Ellerslie.

When Margaret died in 1855, her youngest son, Lewis H. Livingston, inherited the Ellerslie mill. During the ownership by this Livingston, the property underwent some major changes. The northerly portion covering the mill pond remained with Grasmere while the easterly boundary was extended to take in more land east of the Landsman Kill. In 1856, Lewis Livingston sold six acres of land from the southwest corner and west of Mill Road to Nicholas Hoffman. Hoffman conveyed, by a deed dated 1863, these six acres and an adjoining farm to George Van Steenbergh.

The Van Steenberghs arrived in the New York area in the late 1600's. By the early 1700's the name appears in the records of the "Old Dutch Church" in Kingston. Col. Henry Beekman Livingston, the owner of two mills on the Landsman Kill, recruited two Van Steenberghs for his Revolutionary War Regiment. The Rhinebeck

Dutch Reformed Church graveyard has the tomb markers of several Van Steenberghs.

The Van Steenbergh family that bought the farm from Nicholas Hoffman was headed by George (1829-1914) and his wife Elizabeth Wells (1842-1930) They had six children, three sons (George, John, and Wells) and three daughters (Jane, Helen, and Kate). George (1860-1946) and Wells (1868-1944) were the mill operators. Wells was the only family member to marry. Helen died young at age seven. Kate (1865-1947) was a schoolteacher at the one-room schoolhouse at the corner of Mill Road and Morton Road. She taught school for 54 years and bought the mill property in 1916. Jane (1862-1954) was a "craft person," she made a violin from a cherry log and built her own house, which is standing on Mill Road.

In 1857, Lewis Livingston sold the mill site, approximately eight acres of water and land, with a deed containing the wording "with the privilege of the dam and drawing water," to Samuel G. Tripp. It was surveyed by Hazard Champlin in April 1857.[2] This survey follows the property through nine more transactions.

The following years appear to have been difficult financially for the mill operators. The property went through three defaults on mortgage payments and each time, by order of the court, sold at public auction. The auctions were conducted at the Rhinebeck Hotel, now the Beekman Arms.

Tripp sold to the Lueddekes in 1865, who operated the mills up until 1872. It appears that others controlled the property through mortgages, and after several re-financings, it was bought at public auction by the Feller brothers in 1873.[3]

An 1867 map and directory of Rhinebeck businesses lists L. Lueddeke as operating the grist mill and saw mill. He is listed in the Rhinebeck Directory as a dealer in flour. He was both the owner and the miller. An advertisement in the Gazette in August of 1871 announced, "All kinds of grinding attended to." The ad was placed by Louis Lueddeke.

2   RHS. Nancy Kelly. "History of Von Steenberg Mills"
3   DC Clerk–Deed. Liber 139 page 378

The Montgomery/Ellerslie/Van Steenbergh Mills—1774

In February of 1871 a fire destroyed the mill. An article in the Gazette published in April of 1871 stated the mill was being rebuilt and would be back in operation in June. A few weeks later, the Gazette followed with a story that Mr. Alfred Pinder was about to install a "large engine" in the new mill. This new "large engine" was most likely a new water turbine, more efficient than the old water wheel. Pinder built a second mill, a saw and plaster mill, directly across the stream from the flour mill. The shaft of the new "engine" stretched 60 feet across the stream to power the old flour mill, certainly an innovative accomplishment. The paper reported that Pinder was an enterprising, "go-ahead" man and deserved unlimited patronage. The mill opened in August of 1871, a few months behind schedule.

The photo below, taken in 1872, shows the new saw and plaster mill Pinder built on the southwest bank of the Landsman Kill. Perhaps the man in the photo wearing a dark business suit is Alfred Pinder?

Although Pinder is credited with the rebuilding of the mill with its new engine, he did not own the property. Louis Lueddeke was still the owner, most likely employing Pinder as the millwright. In 1872, the owner's mortgage was in default and the mill went to public auction. Peter and John Feller were the buyers of the property. In an April 1872 advertisement in the Gazette, A. Pinder announced he had purchased this well-known mill and was now prepared to offer custom work, flour and feed manufactured to order.[4]

Pinder was expanding his operation. In June of 1874, the Gazette reported that a jury could not reach a decision on the Pinder Mill's request to build a road from the mill to the Hudson River. Pinder did not build his new road. Another name, "Pinder Mill," was introduced for this mill site.

Pinder went "under" five years later, in 1879, when again, the property went to public auction. It was purchased by George W. Shelly.[5]

The Van Steenbergh brothers became the mill operators, under some kind of arrangement with Shelly. They operated the mills for 35 years until this financial arrangement defaulted in 1916. The brothers declared bankruptcy in 1916. George and Wells Van Steenbergh are shown in the U.S. Censuses of 1910 and 1920 as "millers." Their flour was marketed under the trade name of "Garfield" and the logo reads "Pride of Dutchess." The stencil used to mark the flour package has survived and is decorating the wall of a house on Mill Road!

4 Rhinebeck Gazette. Advertisement, August 1, 1874
5 DC Clerk Deed. Liber 273 page 160.

An obituary on the death of Melvin Clearwater stated he was the "proprietor of the Van Steenbergh Mill for several years."[6] The dates for this "proprietor" were not given, making it difficult to determine the time he was employed at the mill.

Kate Van Steenbergh, a schoolteacher at the Morton Road school for 54 years, bought the property at public auction for $6500 in 1916, the same year her brothers declared bankruptcy.

In January of 1918, the Gazette ran a correction notice as follows, "The Van Steenbergh mill, sometimes known as the old Ellerslie mill, is running at the present time. The Gazette wishes to correct the statement in last weeks issue that the mill is not in use at the present." Apparently the Van Steenbergh brothers continued to operate the mill after the 1916 bankruptcy and the purchase of the mill by their sister, Kate.

The photo above, taken by Tracy Dows in 1915, shows a dilapidated mill building, without a water wheel. By this advanced date,

6 Gazette Oct 10, 1931

the mill power was most likely from a water turbine, Pinder's "new engine." A close look at the photo shows the hint of a second building on the far left. This is the remains of the saw and plaster mill added by Pinder in 1871. Footings can still be seen on the west bank where this mill was located.

In 1947, Elizabeth Gray, daughter of Wells Van Steenbergh, was the owner of the mill property. She sold the two mill buildings to Sheldon Burroughs, who dismantled them and reused the material to build a house on Ackert Hook Road.[7]

A photo, undated from the Van Steenbergh collection, shows a horse and carriage crossing the bridge over the waterfall at "Twin Kills." On the left you can see part of the second mill Pinder built to house his saw and plaster mill; on the right is the flour mill.

7 Beverly Burroughs Kane, a volunteer archivist, Rhinebeck Historical Society; conversation and email exchange with author, June 2019.

The Montgomery/Ellerslie/Van Steenbergh Mills—1774

"Twin Kills" is an important mill site, once having two mill buildings and a long history. This site was the last to shut down making it the longest operating mill on the Landsman Kill, from 1774 to at least 1918. Most of the mills on the Landsman Kill ceased operations by the 1870s, at a time when this mill was rebuilt and upgraded.

The remains of both foundations are still visible. This site is so unusual and unique it has been suggested that it be designated and preserved as an archaeological site.

The ownership of this property is tabulated below:

1774 General Richard Montgomery
1785 Col. Henry Livingston.
1812 Christian Schell
1812 General Morgan Lewis
1844 Margaret Lewis Livingston
1855 Lewis H. Livingston
1857 Samuel G. Tripp
1865 Christinna Lueddeke

1869 Pultz, Anson, Feller via mortgages
1872 Alfred Pinder
1879 George W. Shelly via mortgage
1916 Kate Van Steenbergh
1934 Wells P. Van Steenbergh
1946 Elizabeth Gray (daughter of Wells)

The following poem was published in the Rhinebeck Gazette. It was part of an article entitled "Rhinebeck the Beautiful" and written by J. T. Hammick in 1889, and republished in 1931.

> Just below our town stands the Van Steenberg's Mill.
> Having grain of all kinds, all orders can fill:
> Can grind all our grain, supplying each ones needs,
> This to our people is convenient in deed:
> Energetic young men, they work with a will,
> Always kind and ready your orders to fill.

CHAPTER 19

The Isaac Davis Mill
1790–1821

An old stone house, listed with the National Register of Historic Places, sits on the bank of the Landsman Kill and close to the Sepasco Indian trail that is now Route 308. This is the Jan Pier house, built sometime before 1761. It is located across from the present Wonderland Nursery and west of Saltsman's Christmas Tree Farm. In 1790, Isaac Davis acquired the property and built his mill. The deed, dated November 1, 1790, shows he bought 127 acres for 850 pounds. He purchased the property from the Livingston sisters, Janet Montgomery and Margaret Tillotson and her husband Thomas.[1]

Isaac Davis (1745–1821) was a prominent member of the Rhinebeck community. He was a veteran of the Revolutionary War, a Captain in the 4th Regiment of the Militia, and a property owner. Olin Dows, the artist responsible for the Rhinebeck Post Office's mural depicting the history of the area, portrays Isaac Davis as an Elder of the Dutch Church.[2] He can be seen sitting by the steps, with other elders. Like others in the monied class, he was a slaveholder. A snippet of history reports that he purchased a slave, named "Dick," from Col. Henry B. Livingston and then announced his freedom.[3] Davis's daughter married Dr. Abraham Delamater, a prominent Rhinebeck physician. The Delamaters lived in the house until 1848, when, after Davis's death, his estate sold the property to Albert F. Traver.

1 DC Clerk Deed. Liber 45 page 456.
2 Gazette May 12, 1939. Article "Model of Murals at State Institute" Panel 8 by Olin Dows.
3 Gazette May 16, 1973. Article "Early Rhinebeck Books"

A portion of that property is now owned by Tremper Saltsman, a fifth-generation descendant of the Tremper family member who helped build the mill. Another snippet of history tells a story attributed to William Tremper. Tremper was helping Davis build this mill, when he witnessed a slave fight between the kitchen cook and another servant.[4] Apparently it was such an unusual event that it made the newspapers. William Tremper was the father of Jacob L. Tremper who purchased the property from Traver in 1874.

The site is credited with supporting a grist mill, a saw mill, and possibly a gypsum mill. A Gazette newspaper article, published in February 1941, said it was a saw mill.[5] The 1941 Gazette article by Snyder described it as located between the "pumper house" and Cookingham Drive. The "pumper house" refers to part of the village water system that at one time utilized water supplied by wells located in the vicinity of the present-day Village Garage. The village water was pumped to a storage tank near Violet Hill.

Cookingham Drive refers to a road and bridge that crosses the Landsman Kill. This drive is still in existence and runs across the old dam that once formed the mill pond. The drive goes to the Saltsman Christmas Tree Farm. The mill was downstream near the retaining

wall, which is still present, and close to the old Pier house. The information in the Snyder article proved to be quite accurate.

Tremper Saltsman recalls stories, handed down through the Tremper family, of an abandoned water wheel that was left on the property.[6]

Based on the property deeds tracing the owners of

---

4 Gazette May 1, 1919. Article "Jan Peers House—1761"
5 Gazette Feb 13, 1941. Article "James H. Snyder Tells of Past Glories of the Landsman Kill"
6 Author interview with Tremper Saltsman, Jan 11, 2019

The Isaac Davis Mill—1790

the mill site, the mill operated from 1790 until before Isaac Davis's death in 1821.

Records at the Rhinebeck Historical Society show Isaac Davis as a miller and show him collecting "tole" from 1781 through 1783. The records are silent after that.

CHAPTER 20

The Wurtemburg Mill
1790

Morgan Lewis, through his wife's inheritance, controlled a large tract of land east of the Landsman Kill known as Wurtemburg. In 1790 he acquired the rights, from Johannes Van Wagenen, to build a dam across the Landsman Kill.[1] This agreement allowed Lewis to flood the lands he owned east of the stream. It is assumed that Lewis built his first mill before 1800, as in 1801 he bought another "right of way" to access the Hudson River to accommodate his tenants at Wurtemburg. The Garrettsons, part of the Livingston clan, living on a river estate called "Wildercliff," sold him land bordering the Hudson River. He built a dock on the property. By 1850 it was known as Kelly's dock, as it was owned by William Kelly.

In 1792 Lewis built a Staatsburgh home, now the Staatsburgh State Historic Site also known as the Mills Mansion. He and his wife, Gertrude Livingston, had one daughter, who married a Livingston cousin and would later inherit the mills.

Lewis owned three mills on the Landsman Kill, the one he purchased from Col. Henry Livingston, the Wurtemburg Mill, and a later one at Buttermilk Falls.

The mill at Wurtemburg was a grist mill serving his tenants who were required to pay their rents in wheat. Records at the Staatsburgh Historic Site contain tenant names and the number of bushels of wheat the miller collected for General Lewis. In 1830, some thirty tenants paid a total of 460 bushels of wheat to Jacob Briggs, most

1 Gazette June 9, 1894. Articles "The Kip Bergen Families"

likely the miller. In 1825, the receiver of rents was George Briggs, no doubt related. The Rhinebeck 1850 Census lists a George Briggs as a miller.

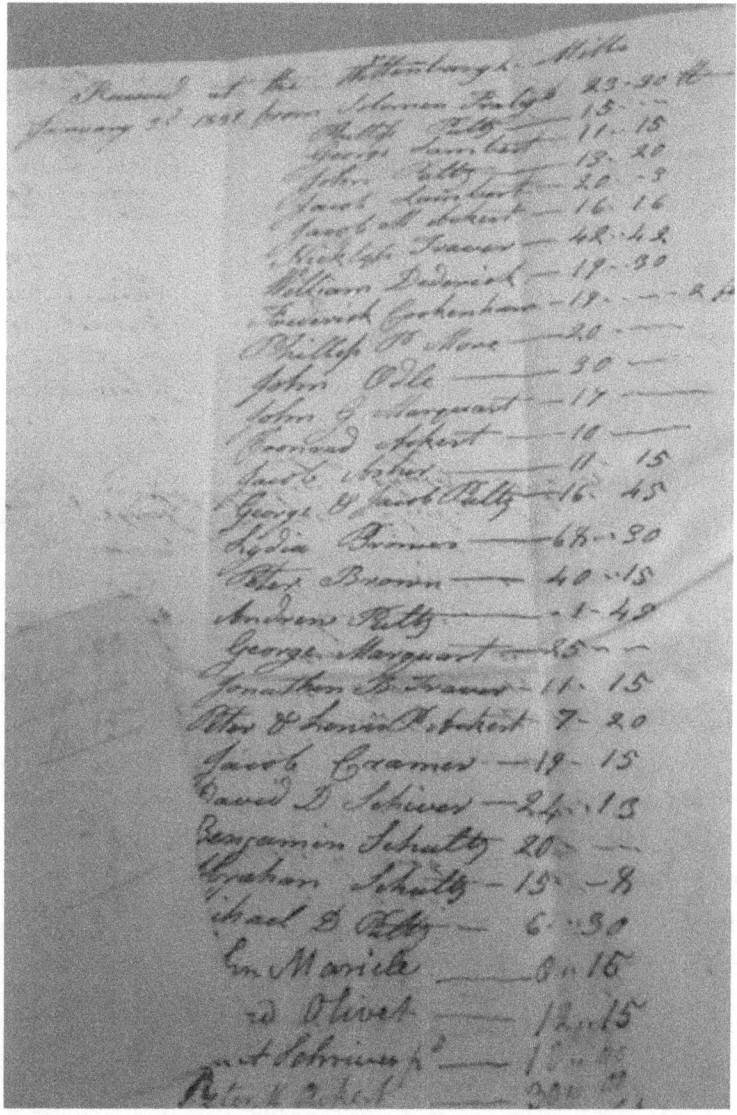

A typical entry from the records reads as follows: "March 17 1825 Received in Wurtemburg Mill from John R Ostram twenty three bushels of wheat rent for M. Lewis by George Briggs,"

Another receipt, from John Ackert for seventeen bushels, is dated December 1824.

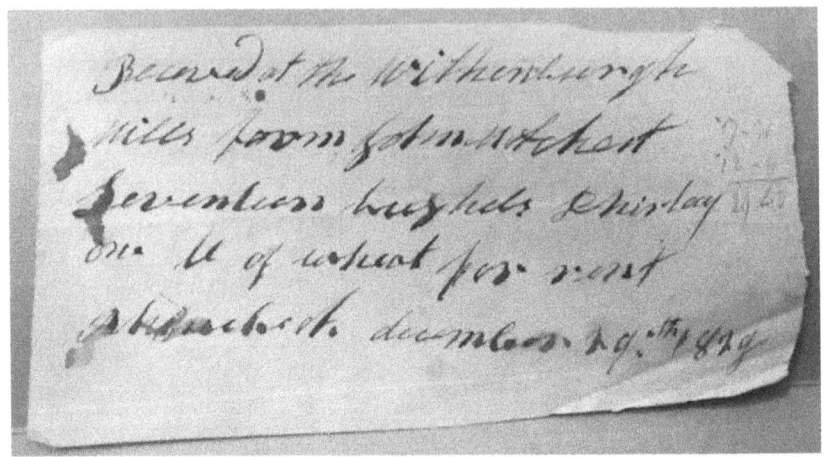

Morse, in his Historic Old Rhinebeck published in 1908, states that this location operated a grist mill, a saw mill, and a woolen mill.[2] It was called a fulling mill in one record.[3] "Daddy" Morrison operated the woolen mill. Coyle was a miller there. The Coyle family farm was owned by Lewis Livingston in 1860.

During the War of 1812, General Morgan Lewis allowed his tenants, those who served in the military or had sons who served, free rent for their time of service. It was a nice gesture.

In various Gazette newspaper articles, and in Morse, the mill location is referred to as "Fox Hollow," a name associated with the Dows property. No archaeological remains of the mill have been found. The bridge over the Landsman Kill that connected the Wurtemburg community to the Hudson River was in use up until the 1950s. The bridge abutments are visible, but the bridge is gone.

2 Morse page 57
3 Dutchess County, New York Geneology and History Chapter XIII—Historic Homes: County Estates

The Wurtemburg Mill—1790

In 1889, Robert Suckley installed a hydro-electric plant at Wilderstein, using water-power to provide electricity to his property.[4] The location of this site is a few yards north of the Wurtemburg bridge. Suckley had a new dam built specifically to power the turbine. It was not built on the old mill site.

---

4 Author interview Wilderstein, Duane Watson curator, Nov 25, 2018

CHAPTER 21

Buttermilk Falls

This spectacular location, with its sixty-foot falls, is now the site of a beautiful architecturally-designed home. There is limited archaeological evidence of its former use as a mill site. A few stone remains are probably associated with the mill buildings. They are located on the east side of the Landsman Kill on property that was owned by Morgan Lewis. An 1867 DeBeers map shows the name as "High Falls" and notes that it is sixty feet.

It is reported that Morgan Lewis operated a paper mill on this site during his lifetime. This is one of three mills that Morgan Lewis operated on the Landsman Kill. A 1798 map of Rhinebeck shows an oil mill at this location. Lewis's papers, at the Staatsburgh State Historic Site, provide no information on this mill.

Buttermilk Falls

A manifest of a New York-bound ship leaving from Long Dock at Rhinecliff, lists 34 bundles of paper from the local paper mill. The date is 1817. The Upper Mill at Crystal Lake converted to produce paper when Hogan purchased the property in 1847. So this consignment of paper was from the Buttermilk Falls mill site.

There is no record of when the mill was built or when it stopped operating.

After the mills were long gone, in the early 1930s, the site had a hydro-electric-generating plant that was operated as a hobby by a local engineer. Today it is the site of a beautiful house, with the structure extending out over the falls.

CHAPTER 22

The Schuyler Mills
?–1888

On the east end of the Landsman Kill, a few hundred yards west of the Rutsen/Schuyler mills, is the site of a woolen mill. Its present location is behind the Staley Real Estate office on Route 308 near the 9G overpass.

There is not a waterfall in this area, so the "head" to drive the wheel must have been from a dam and mill pond. Perhaps the water wheel was an "undershot." Knick Staley reported that the water wheel was located on the right bank, mounted on a stone wall. The wall is gone, washed away by Hurricane Irene in 2011. There are no archaeological remains to identify the exact location of the mill house.

The woolen mill would have been a carding mill. Its purpose was to align the wool fibers so they could be spun into yarn. The mill would have contained a carding machine, invented in England in 1748. The first carding machine was introduced in this area in 1803 by George Booth of Poughkeepsie.[1] The 1840s were a time known for the conversion of grist mills to woolen mills. So this mill was probably placed in operation well after the invention came to the United States. It is probable that this mill began in the mid-1800s. The date the mill was built is not known but it was in operation as late as 1888, the second-longest-operating mill on the Landsman Kill.

An 1876 advertisement in the Gazette announced an offering to sell the woolen mill referred to as "Schuyler's Mills" along with a grist and plaster mill and the machinery connected therewith. The

1 DC–1858–Reference. RHS 2007–027

ad was placed by Joshua S. Bowne, as Executor. Bowne, a prominent businessman, was one of the founders of the Rhinebeck Savings Bank and the President from 1872 until 1876. He was related to the Rutsen/Sands family and thus back to the Beekmans.

> **THE WOOLEN MILL,**
>
> known as "Schuyler's Mills," also the
>
> **GRIST AND PLASTER MILLS,**
>
> and the machinery connected therewith; together with a
>
> **DWELLING HOUSE AND BARN**
>
> and about one acre of land. Situated one mile and a half east of the village of Rhinebeck, on the Delaware and Ulster turn ike, will be offered for sale at the Rhinebeck Hotel, in the village of Rhinebeck, Dutchess county, N. Y., on the 21st day of April next at 11 o'clock, A. M.
>
> **TERMS OF SALE LIBERAL**
>
> and will be made known on the day of sale. March 29, 1876. JOSHUA S. BOWNE, Executor.
> For further particulars enquire of JOSHUA S. BOWNE or of ESSELSTYN & McCARTY, Rhinebeck, N. Y.
> 1t70ts

A Gazette article by James H. Snyder, published in 1941, states that there was a gypsum mill at the same site using the same flume. He did not mention the grist mill. Jim Snyder's article listing the mills on the Landsman Kill appears to be very accurate, and the 1876 ad verified his statement that two mills were operated by the same flume at this location, a fact that could not be verified until finding the 1876 advertisement.

There is no record of who purchased the property but a Gazette advertisement in March of 1888 presented another offering for the sale of the "Old Schuyler Mill property," with the request to "apply on the premises." The ad was placed by Frank Kolbinskee. So the mill was in operation for twelve years after the first offer of sale in 1876. The chain of ownership is not known until 1907, when Frank I Teal, a local Rhinebeck surveyor, mapped and described the property. Map number 1722 is filed with the Dutchess County Clerk's Office. The deeds in the DC Clerk's Office show no transactions for this property. Since the property remained with the Schuyler descendants it can be assumed the "offer for sale" was not consummated.

This property, however, was owned by Grace Sands Montgomery when she died on Feb 15, 1921. Her daughter, Margaret Montgomery Anderson, inherited the property and sold it to Homer K. Staley in 1954. It is the present location of the Staley Real Estate office.

CHAPTER 23

The Forbes Saw Mill

In Jim Snyder's Gazette article in 1941, he mentions the location of a saw mill, "just east of Forbes place." An 1850 Rhinebeck map confirms an "S Mill" at this location. The Gazette article and map are the only references to this mill.

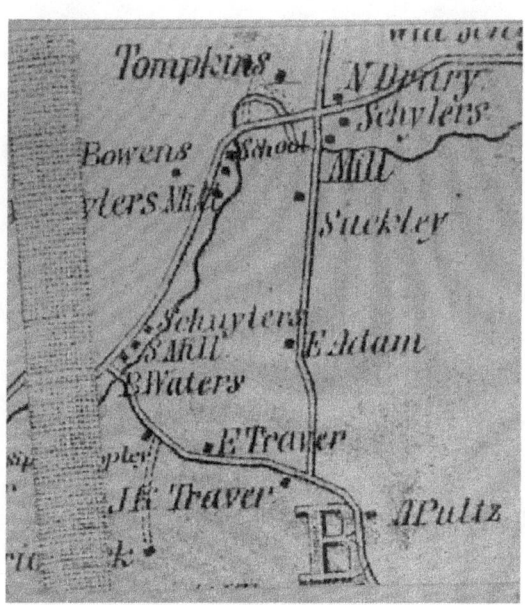

The Forbes property used as a reference for this site was not on the Landsman Kill. It was located on a small hill on the west side of Route 308 just east of Violet Hill Road. On an 1858 map of Dutchess County,[1] the location is called a "turning mill." This is

1

an unknown term for a water-powered mill. Perhaps it refers to a wood-turning operation associated with a furniture manufacturing operation. There were reported to be several furniture operations in Rhinebeck.[2]

The woolen and paper mills, built or converted in the mid-1800s, appear to have had a difficult time financially. Compared with the grist and saw mills, they were relatively short-lived.

---

2 Gazette March 26, 1922. Article "The Old Post Road"

CHAPTER 24

The Important Miller

The miller was a key man for the operation of the grist mill. He had to keep the machinery running and ensure a good, quality product.

In addition to maintaining the water wheel and gearing and dressing the millstones, he had to produce a quality product. The key to a quality product was the adjustment of the height of the runner stone. Too large a gap resulted in a "mushy" product and a too-close gap produced an "off-color" or burnt product.

A common breakdown was an accident allowing the runner stone to touch the bed stone. This caused too much heat and the cracking of the millstone, a major loss.

The miller was constantly checking the clearance of the two stones, keeping his nose to the grind stone!

Because the miller's job was so important, the miller was an important member of the community. The millers were well-compensated, usually by taking a fee for milling a farmer's wheat or trading his flour. The account books of miller Hendrick Denker, from 1735 to 1772, depict the miller as a major merchant. He bartered for all sorts of merchandise, trading flour for clothing, shoes, and even butter. His activities resembled that of a general store owner.

Records show that some millers were able to lease the mill from the owner, instead of being employed. They must have felt they could get more compensation by being independent.

CHAPTER 25

Fire Hazards

Both the saw mill and the grist mill operations were susceptible to fires.

A dust explosion is defined as a rapid combustion of fine particles suspended in air. The ignition can be caused by static electricity or a spark. Both these types of mills could produce fine dust particles.

Flour dust is especially troublesome as it can easily be suspended in air. There are five components to a dust explosion. A concentration of fine particles, suspended in air, in a confined space, having sufficient oxygen, and a source of ignition. Concentrations of 75 to 1000 grams per cubic meter of air are dangerous.

In May of 1876, the Washington "A" mill in Minneapolis, MN, the largest grain mill in the world, exploded, killing 22 people.[1] This is the worst milling accident recorded.

The Landsman Kill had its problems with fires. The Upper Mill, Lower Mill, and "Twin Kills" Mill all burned.

1 https://en.wikipedia.org/wiki/dust_explosion

CHAPTER 26

Social Life at The Mills

A 1908 article in the Rhinebeck Gazette records the reminiscences of an old resident who came to the Flatts in 1828. He talks fondly about the old mill which had been destroyed by fire. He laments, "Another old landmark is gone." "The old mill was known to our early childhood, the picturesque old mill whose vicinity was the scene of so many of our sports in years gone by – of swimming, of fishing, and shall I confess it, much delightful flirting."

Dewitt Gurnell, The Rhinebeck historian in the 1960s, wrote about the existence of "Lovers Lane"[1] near the mill site. He told of "a winding lane, lined with rose bushes which led to Montgomery Mills," the longest-operating mills in Rhinebeck's history.

A mural, painted by Rhinebeck's Olin Dows on the south wall of the Rhinebeck Post Office, depicts a scene of swimmers at the mill pond. A large water wheel is in the background.

The entire mural tells the story of Rhinebeck's early history, with scenes depicting the Kip's buying the first land rights from the Indians, to Col. Henry Beekman collecting his rents at the old Kip House in Rhinecliff. Olin Dows stated that the mill pond represented a "composite" of the Beekman and Montgomery mills. The mills were a significant part of the town's history and he included them in the mural.

The Rhinebeck Town emblem displays two foreign flags (Dutch and English), and a mill wheel, reflecting the importance of the mills in Rhinebeck's history.

1 History of Rhinebeck—Hon Dewitt Gurnell Town Historian Pamphlet, RHS

Rhinebeck and the History of the Landsman Kill Mills

Social Life at The Mills

The romantic theme of the reminiscences of the old resident in the Gazette article was felt throughout the country. A bestselling piece of music from 1908, composed by Tell Taylor, sold a record four million copies. The song became a staple of barber shop quartets for many years after.

Do you remember these lyrics?

> My darling I am dreaming of the days gone by
> When you and I were sweet hearts beneath the summer sky'
> Your hair has turned silver, the gold has faded too,
> But still I will remember where I first met you.
>
> The old mill wheel is silent and has fallen down,
> The old oak tree has weathered and lies there on the ground,
> While you and I were sweethearts the same as days of yore,
> Although we've been together forty years or more.
>
> Down by the old mill stream, where I first met you,
> With your eyes of blue, dressed in gingham too,
> It was there I knew that you loved me true,
> You were sixteen, my village queen, by the old mill stream.

CHAPTER 27

The Rhinebeck Millstone

In June of 2018, the Rhinebeck Highway Department discovered a 3000-pound chunk of stone when they were digging to replace an old culvert. The stone was a grist stone, a 57-inch runner stone from some forgotten and abandoned grist mill. It was cleaned up and displayed in front of the Highway Department's building and drew the attention of local historians. The stone was studied, measured, analyzed, photographed, and written about. It was, indeed, a valuable find and the Department should be afforded credit for preserving a piece of Rhinebeck's history.

Inspection of the millstone afforded a unique opportunity to review the history of the grist mill and its importance to the economic well-being of Rhinebeck in the mid-1700s. As this article suggests, the grist mill was the main source of revenue for all but two of the ten Landsman Kill mills.

The discovery initiated local interest in the grist mill and residents volunteered information on the location of other stones, some hidden along the bank of the Kill and others displayed as private trophies. Many of the photos of mill stones in this article are the result of that activity.

The Rhinebeck Millstone shows the unique "lands and furrows" of grist stone. The grist mill employs two identically matched stones, one permanently mounted, the bed stone, and one rotating, the runner stone. The grooves, dressed by the miller, leave a "signature" unique to that miller. These marks can be used to trace the identity of the pair.

Rhinebeck Mill Stones

Prepared by Town Historian
Nancy Kelly

Tan Stone, found by Highway Dept Slate Quarry Rd near Wurtemburg origin unknown (Schuyler Mil?) Jacob Rutsen built mill 1744 *Morse p233*

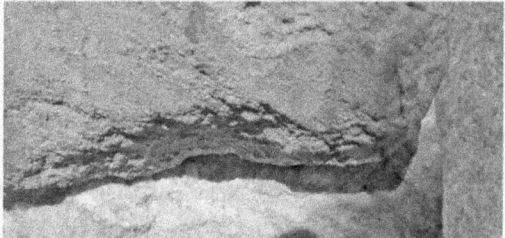

Gray Stone from Beekman Lower Milll, Astor Home on display at Quitman House. Mill c.1750 (Traphagen)

Gray Stone from Red Hook Mill on display Cedar Heights Scribe ines are similar to Quitman stone

The Rhinebeck Millstone is 57 inches in diameter and 8 inches thick. It is made from grey Shawangunk Quartz Conglomerate manufactured locally near High Falls in Ulster County. It is an Esopus stone. It is capable of producing 500 pounds of wheat flour per hour.

This stone is cracked, making it unusable and probably why it was abandoned. A common cause of cracking was overheating. The miller allowed the two stones to touch, with the friction building enough heat to destroy the stone. Was this a mechanical accident or inattention? The miller's job is to produce a quality product by adjusting the gap between the two stones.

The miller had a critical skill to keep the mill in operation. "Keeping your nose to the grind stone" is an appropriate job description!

The challenge is to find a mate for this Rhinebeck runner stone.

CHAPTER 28

Millstones Today

There is a market for these old antiques. The internet lists prices from $3000 to as high as $5000 dollars for stones to be used for landscaping or other decorative works. Several stones are locally displayed, some at institutions, some privately, and some abandoned.

For example, Bard College's Montgomery Place campus has a 37-inch runner stone mounted as a decorative piece in front of the Carriage House.

Marist College discovered three stones during the excavation for the renovated Art Center. These stones have been artistically-mounted in the floor of the new building, complete with back lightning, and displayed as an art piece. These stones are probably grindstones as the circular markings are associated with this product. The grindstones were probably used to shape metal and would be associated with the steel plant operations.

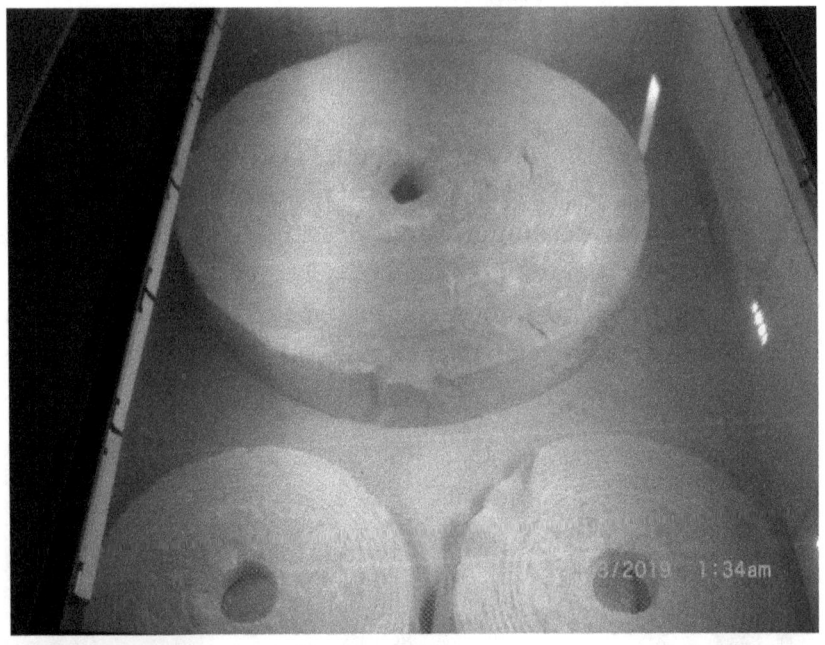

Millstones Today

The Quitman House Museum, located behind the Old Stone Church established by the Palatines, has a 57-inch bed stone on display. It was donated by the Astor Home for Children and is from the Lower Mill site.

Don McTernan, a Trustee with the Rhinebeck Historical Society and former Chief Curator at the Home of FDR and Vanderbilt Mansion, part of the National Park Service, in Hyde Park provided the following photo of an abandoned millstone.

It is located near the Rutsen/Schuyler/Miller site on property that belonged to the Sands family. Named the "Sand's Millstone" it is a "runner stone" measuring 48 inches in diameter and 7 inches thick. The eye hole is 9 inches in diameter with four 3 inch notches to receive the "rind." The "rind" is a metal insert that attaches the runner tone to the rotating shaft.

Above: Grist Stone from Beekman's Lower Mill
Below: The Sand's Millstone

Two stones are displayed at a private home on Cedar Heights Road. The larger millstone is a fifty-inch bed stone, 7 inches thick with a classic pattern of furrows and grooves. The source is one of the Red Hook Mills, not the Landsman Kill. The smaller stone, 22 inches in diameter and 4 inches thick, is probably a stone from an oil mill. It has no furrows but a smooth circumference indicative of a roller stone.

This millstone found in an abandoned grist mill near Pine Plains is a French Burr stone. It is not manufactured from a solid piece of granite but is a composite of material cemented together. This is a highly-prized millstone for milling flour.

The Rhinebeck Millstone on display at the Rhinebeck Highway Department garages.

APPENDIX A

Casper Landsman

The name Lampman and Landman seem to be used interchangeably in the old records. This family is found on the Stone Church Family List of 1734 (St. Peter's Evangelical Lutheran Church, Rhinebeck). We expect that Beekman papers in archives such as the NY Historical Society and Princeton Library's Edward Livingston Collection will confirm the suspicion that the Landsman Kill was named for Casper Landman/Lampman. The Family List confirms that he was living in Rhinebeck at an early date and probably functioned as Beekman's miller at the mill on the mouth of the Landsman Kill. Historian James Smith relates that Casper was engaged to help engineer the mill and act as miller. References show that Henry Beekman set up his mill in 1710 prior to the settlement of Palatines in Rhinebeck. Casper may have been responsible for locating later mill sites on the stream. Perhaps the mill at The Flatts was his handiwork.

As was commonly true, Palatines settled here by the English Crown were reluctant to be unfaithful to the King. The Livingston Committee of Safety reported that Hendrik and Casper Lampman were among those who were said to have signed the "King's Book, and huzzah for the King."

Later, the brothers fought for the rebellion and were taken prisoners. Casper is on the 1779 Personal Property and Real Estate Tax List for Livingston Manor. He may have been living near the grist and saw mills located between Gattatin and Acram on the Roeliff Jansen Kill.

Casper's father, Peter, was the Palatine Emigrant (Palatine Families of NY, 1710 #429 p.514). On July 7, 1698 he received a permit to go to Stockheim where he married. This permit was located at the Castle of Ortenberg in record book Akte X G 436 p. 9. He was naturalized, Albany Co. 1716 on the Simmindinger List at Wormsdorf, a Palatine Debtor 1718,19,21 & b26 lists. He signed as one who wished to remain on the Livingston Manor 1724 and is listed on the Stone Church Family List, Rhinebeck in 1734.

—Nancy Kelly, RHS

APPENDIX B

∼

Deeds and the Beekman Mills

Several land transactions were recorded between the Beekmans and Traphagens. The first was in 1705 when Henry Beekman of Ulster County sold 281 acres to William Traphagen, a wheelwright from Kingston. In 1719, Traphagen returned six acres to Beekman, reportedly to correct the property lines of Beekman's 1715 mill. Later, in 1746, a land swap added two and a third acres to Beekman's six and gave Traphagen an additional acre and a half.

The first transaction in 1705 was not recorded in the Dutchess County Clerk's Office until 1741. See Liber 1 page 380. It was typical in colonial times to wait years before recording these transactions.

The second transaction, the 1719 return of six acres, was recorded in 1770, but dated in 1746. See Liber 5 page 399. This record is accompanied by a map describing the six acres plus the land swap. The map shows the presence of a mill and dam. There is a document, among the papers of Edward Livingston in the Princeton University archives, that shows an agreement between the sons of Beekman and Traphagen, dated 1719. This document has a similar description of the property lines of the six-acre transaction, except it refers to the "falls" without reference to the "mill dam." This paper was never recorded in the Dutchess County Clerk's Office, but the Deed in Liber 5 makes reference to that 1719 sale.

The wording of this deed, Liber 5, page 399, is as follows:

> "Lands possessed in Rhynbeek Precinct granted by Lord Cornberry unto Col Henry Beekman of Ulster Co deceased and since is become the inheritance of Henry Beekman party

Appendix B: Deeds and the Beekman Mills

to these presents and whereas William father to said Arent Traphagen in his lifetime stood possessed of 281 acres of land conveyed by said Col Henry Beekman late of Ulster County – deceased to said William Traphagen deceased dated 1705, and on the first day of Jan 1719, the said William Traphagen by conveyance sold and made over unto Henry Beekman six acres thereof to be taken from the southeast angle by the sale of water for the conveneancy to erect mills thereon and the same Arent Traphagen stands possessing according to the will of his father."

Part of the description of the six acres boundaries follows:

"Beginning on the falls near the mill dam where the first marked tree stood – thence ---- to stone set on west side of the Kings high road – thence unto a hollow by a rivulet of water mid stream---."

The map, part of this Deed, is shown below.

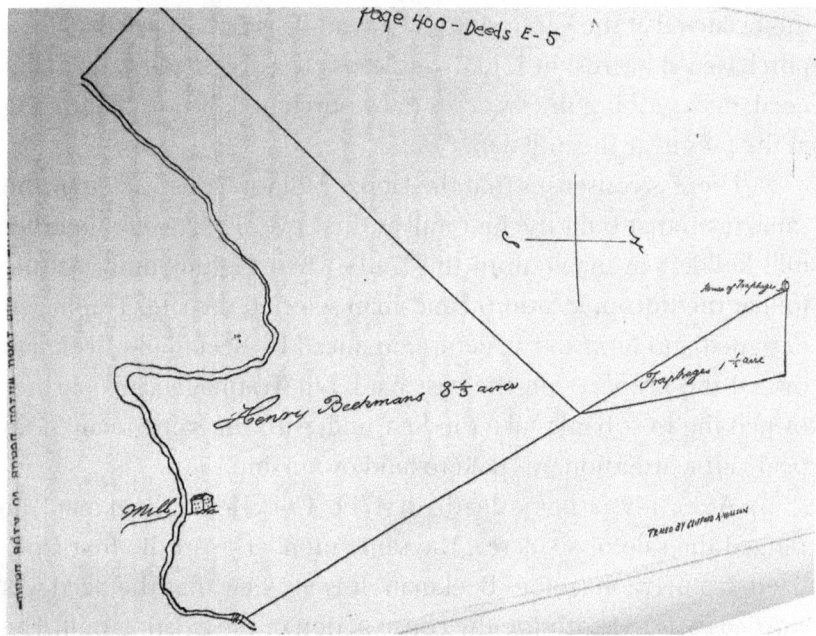

85

APPENDIX C

∼

A Case for the 1715 Mill Date

The reference to the 1719 transfer of six acres to Beekman for the purpose of erecting a mill thereon, calls into question the date the Upper Mill was constructed.

It is my premise that this six-acre land transfer was to insure the property lines of the already existing mill were legally recognized.

1) The Landsman Kill was an inconvenient boundary between the two major patents. The lands in question were not occupied, with no one to question a violation of property rights. By definition, a dam had to cross the two banks, and if one side was not owned by the dam builder, an obvious legal problem existed. It appeared that this occurred at the Vanderburgh Cove mill, as Col. Henry Beekman purchased six acres, in 1710, from Roosa to correct the error. That deed, in describing the six acres to be purchased, began "beginning at the falls near the mill dam." etc.

2) There is consensus that the Upper Mill was constructed by the same team that built the first mill at the Cove. There were no other mill builders available until the 1740's when Eighmy built a stone mill at the Rutsen location. Landsman selected the site, Traphagen designed and built the structure, financed by Beekman. Beekman owned the property on the east bank but Traphagen, his partner, owned the west bank. Like the first mill, with the same team, it appears little attention was paid to land ownership.

3) After his father's death in 1719, Col. Henry Beekman, arranged the sale of six acres, the same number as in the first Cove deed, from Traphagen to Beekman. It is my view that the deed was worded so as to legitimize the construction of the existing mill. The

recorded deed, Liber 1, page 399, uses similar language as the Cove deed, e.g. "beginning at the falls of the mill dam", etc. See details in Appendix B.

4) Beekman needed the mill to support the rents of the 35 families he brought to Pink's Corners from the failed Naval Stores project at Clermont. The date of this migration was 1715. The timing supports the 1715 date for the Upper Mill.

5) The 1715 date was published by three historians, Morse, Smith, and Hasbrouck. It is agreed they offered no specific reference to support that date. The only possible challenge is the wording in the Princeton document, which can be explained.

6) The preponderance of circumstantial facts supports the 1715 date for the Upper Mill.

REFERENCES

1: Morse, Howard Holdridge, "Historic old Rhinebeck," Pocontico Printery, Tarrytown-on-Hudson, NY 1908
2: Smith, James H., "History of Dutchess County," D. Mason Co, 1882
3: Hasbrouck, Frank, "The History of Dutchess County, New York," S.A. Matthieu, Poughkeepsie, NY 1909
4: The Rhinebeck Gazette, J.H. Strong, Editor, various issues.
5: Rhinebeck Historical Society, (RHS) Rhinebeck, NY, Starr Library record room.
6: Dutchess County Clerk's Office, Poughkeepsie, NY, Record Room - Deeds - Maps
7: Wilderstein Historic Site, Duane Watson, Curator of Collections.
8: Nancy Kelly, Rhinebeck Town Historian.
9: Beverly Burroughs Kane, a volunteer archivist, Rhinebeck Historical Society; conversation and email exchange with author, June 2019.

ABOUT THE AUTHOR

∼

Jack Conklin is a retired businessman living in Rhinecliff, New York, in a restored 1860 house overlooking the beautiful Hudson River. He grew up on a family dairy farm near Pleasant Valley, NY, attended local schools and graduated from USMA, West Point with the Class of 1956. His Army experience includes duty as an Infantry Officer, Paratrooper, Army Pilot, Staff Officer with 4 years assigned to the 101st Airborne Division at Fort Campbell, Kentucky.

After the military, Jack was employed as a Project Engineer with Procter and Gamble in Cincinnati, Ohio. He built the first "Downy" pilot plant and installed the first "Pampers" test market line. He returned to Dutchess County and joined the DeLaval Separator Company as a sales engineer, and after a succession of challenging assignments became President in 1975.

Following DeLaval, Jack was associated with several local businesses as a board member or owner, including Standard Gage, Fargo, Dutchess Bank, Chief Electronics, and Discount Data Products.

In retirement, his interest in local history afforded an opportunity to write a "history" column for two local newspapers and publish several articles for the Dutchess County and Rhinebeck Historical Societies.

This is his second published book on local history.

www.ingramcontent.com/pod-product-compliance
Lightning Source LLC
Chambersburg PA
CBHW070654050426
42451CB00008B/342